I Like to Read

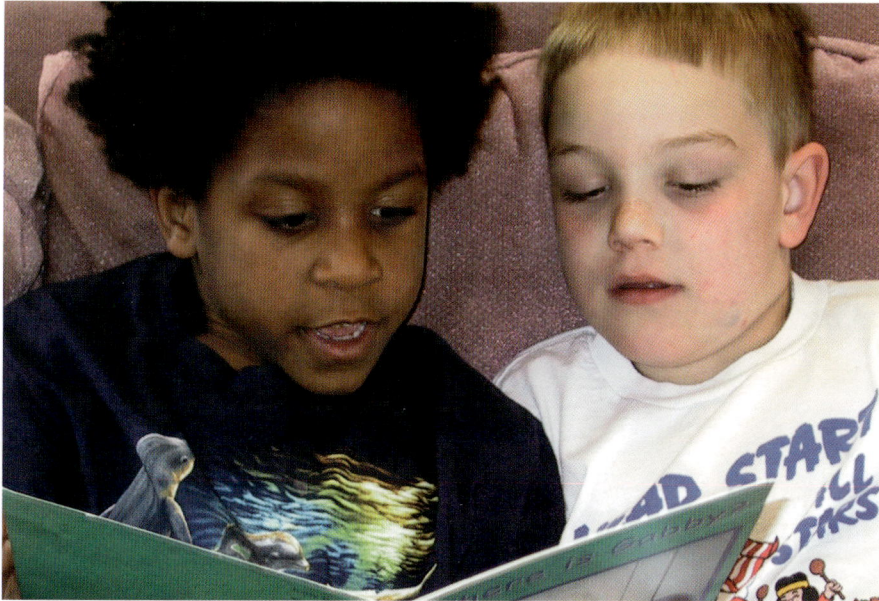

by Michèle Dufresne

Pioneer Valley Educational Press, Inc.

I like to read.

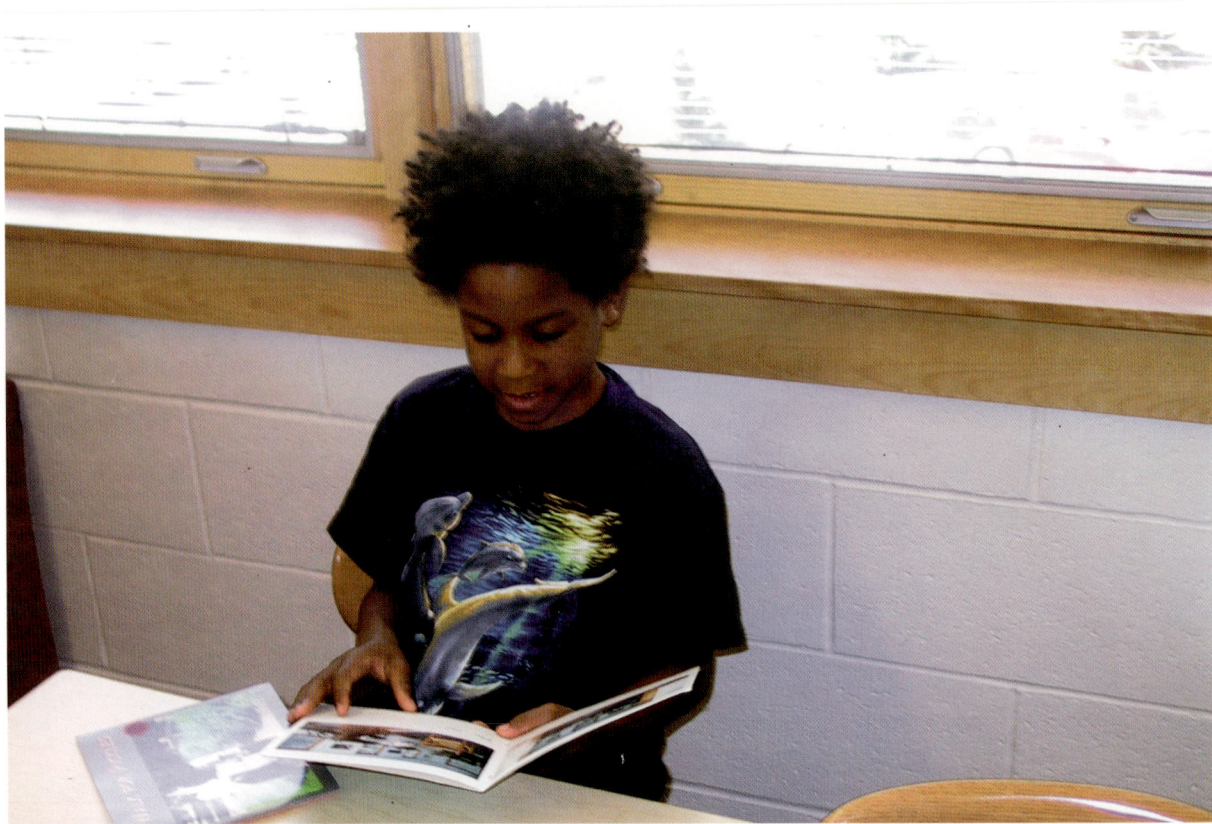

I like to read to my friend.

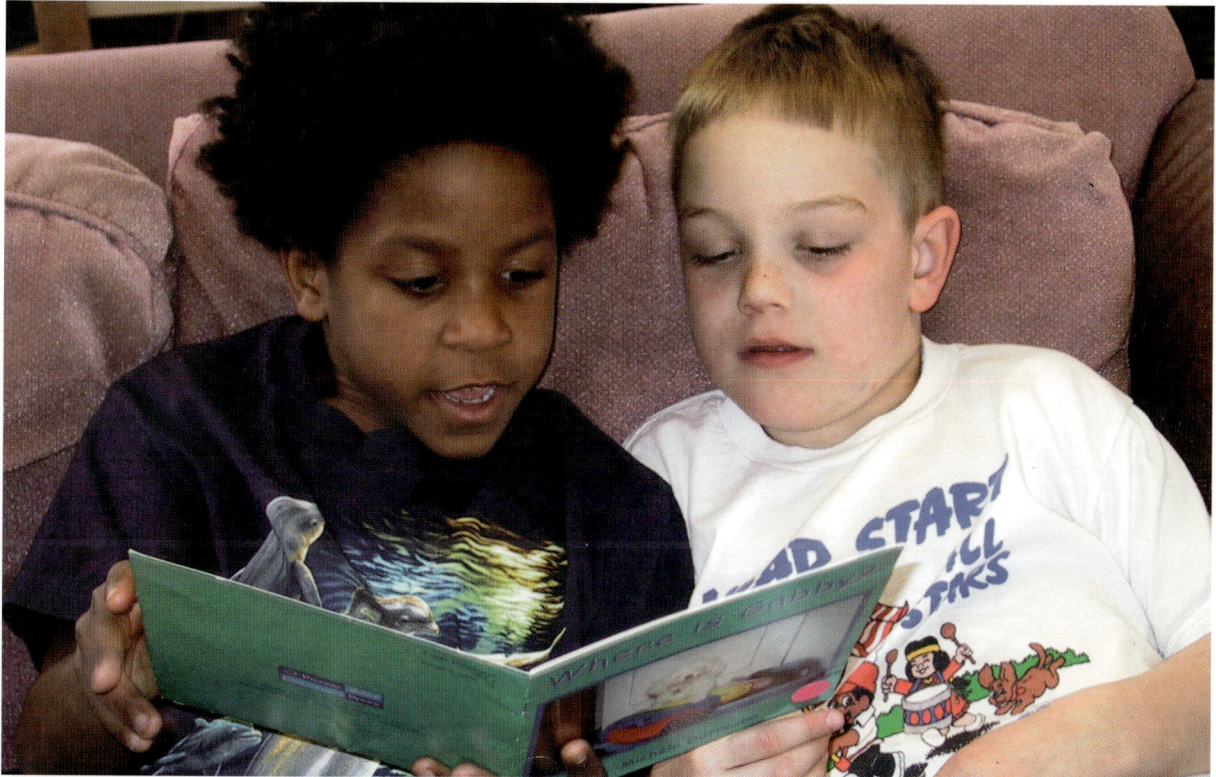

I like to read to my dinosaur.

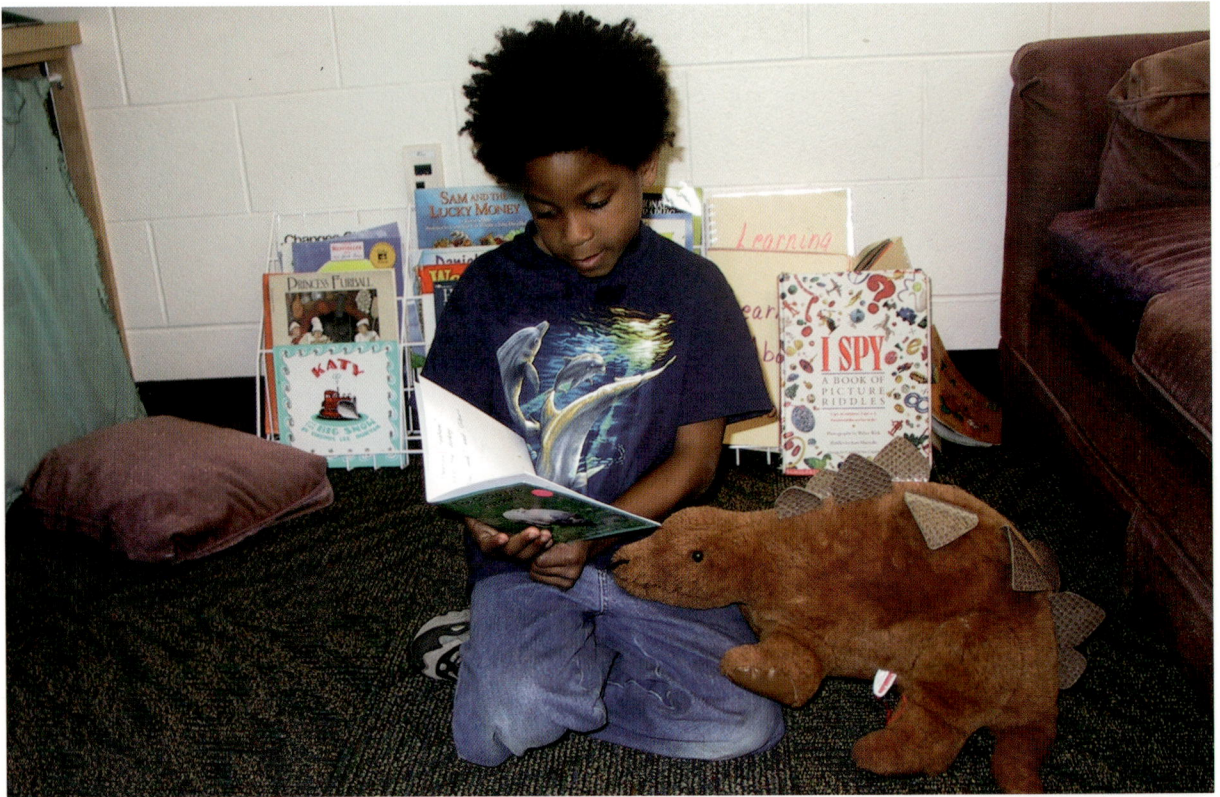

I like to read to my teacher.

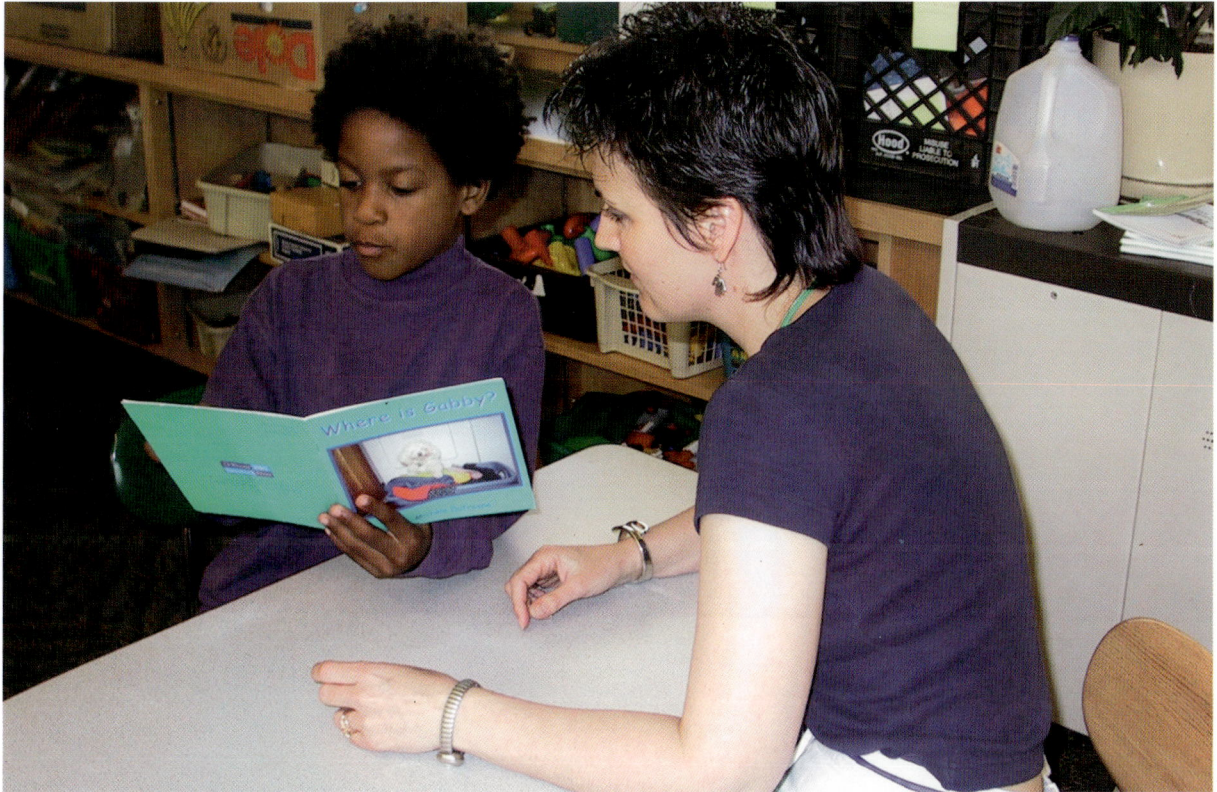

I like to read to my teddy bear.

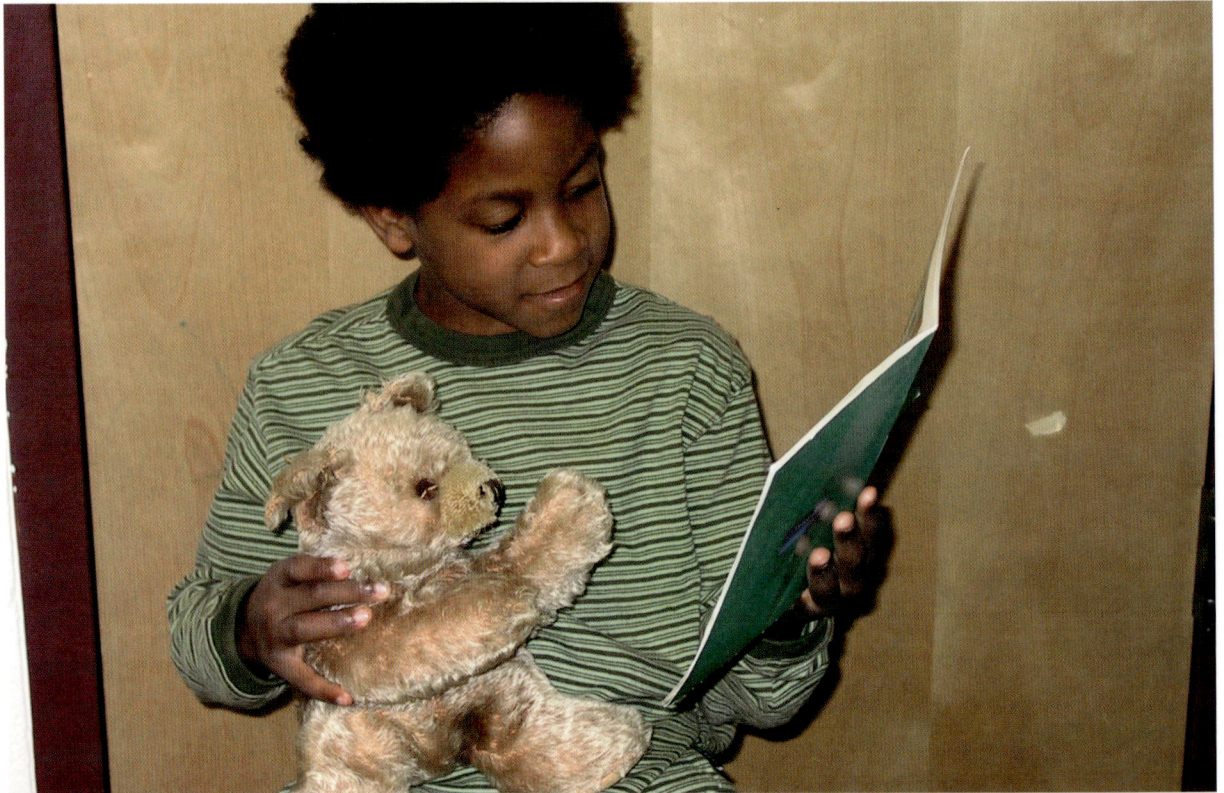

I like to read to my dog.

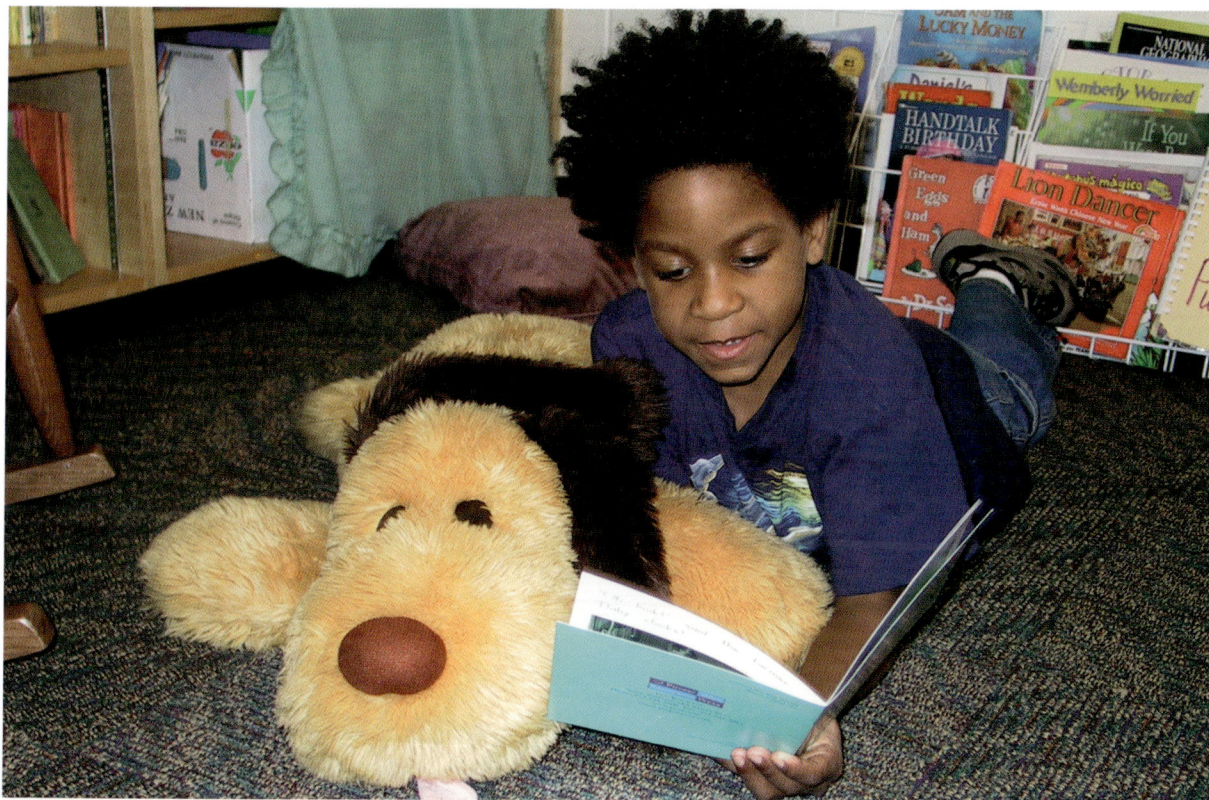

I like to read!

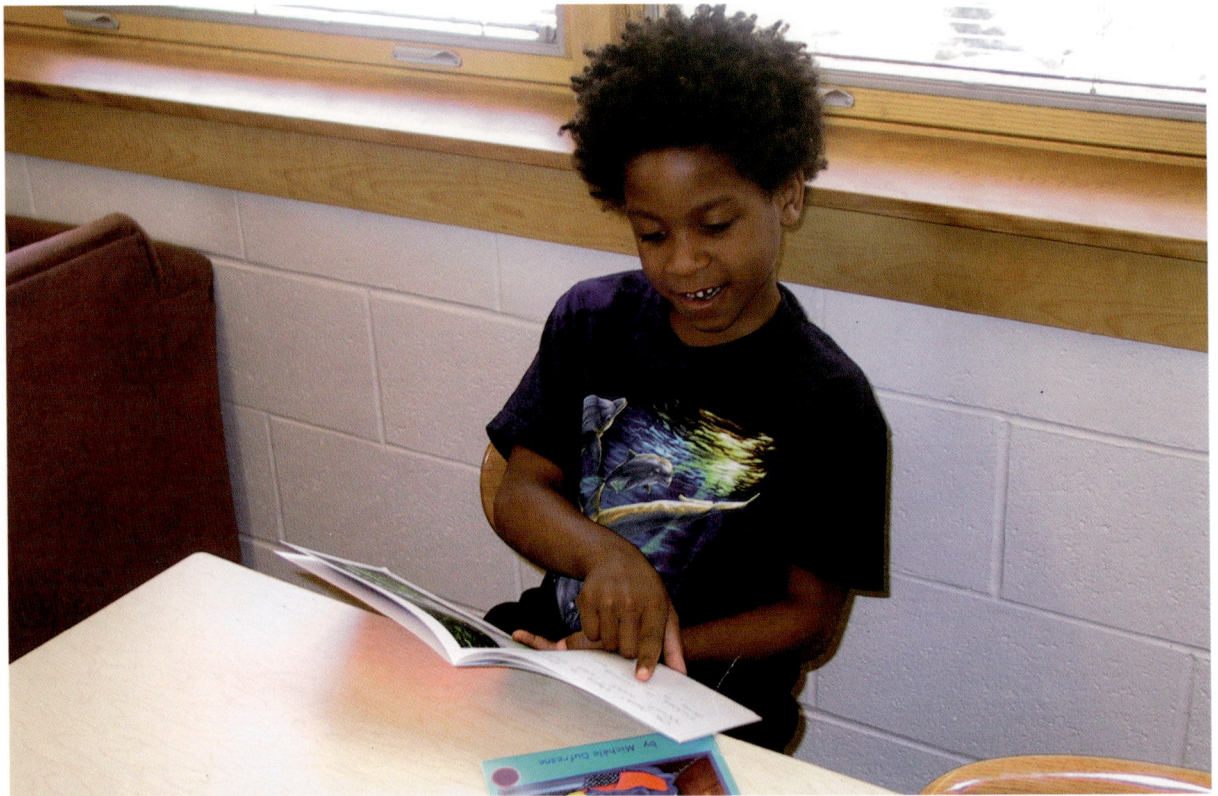